ENGLAND EXPECTS
The Battle of Sluys

GORDON CORRIGAN

© Gordon Corrigan, 2016

Gordon Corrigan has asserted his rights under the Copyright, Design and Patents Act, 1988, to be identified as the author of this work.

First published by Endeavour Press Ltd in 2016.

ISBN: 9781726789189

CONTENTS

INTRODUCTION

1 — Plantagenet England

2 — Preparations for War

3 — To War

4 — Into Battle

5 — The Battle That Changed History

ENGLAND EXPECTS
The Battle of Sluys

INTRODUCTION

Few battles actually change history. For all the posturing by the victors and excuses by the losers, a different result for most clashes of arms would not often have substantively altered what was actually to happen anyway. Had Nelson lost at Trafalgar the Royal Navy could have withstood the loss of twenty-seven ships of the line, and while total dominance of the seas by Britain might have taken a little longer, it would still have come, and in any case the French 'Army of England', poised to invade, had been marched off to Germany well before Trafalgar.

Waterloo is a famous British battle, but if Napoleon and not Wellington had won it, Napoleon would nevertheless have lost the war, for while Britain's defeated army might have scuttled back to England, her government would have continued to finance the seventh coalition and the enormous Russian, Austrian and Prussian armies converging on Paris would still have put paid to the Napoleonic dream.

A reverse at Second Alamein, much trumpeted as a great British victory, would not have altered the course of the war – Rommel and his Panzer Army Africa had been written off by

Berlin, could receive no reinforcements and was short of everything from vehicles to ammunition to socks. The North African campaign might have taken a bit longer, but the eventual result would have been the same.

For a battle to change history we must be able to demonstrate unequivocally that a different result would have fundamentally and irrevocably altered what was to come. Also there must have been a realistic possibility that the outcome could have been different. As an example, if Operation Sea Lion, the projected German invasion of England in 1940 had succeeded, history would have been changed utterly. We cannot, however, consider it as a battle that changed history because there was never the slightest possibility of German success, for even if the Germans had managed to establish air superiority over the Channel in the first phase, the Battle of Britain, invasion was completely impossible – the Germans did not have the equipment, the landing craft or the naval assets to do it, as they (and the British government) knew very well. Sluys, the subject of this book, was different. It was fought in 1340 and was one of the opening battles of what came to be called the Hundred Years War. While most history buffs know about Crécy, Poitiers and Agincourt, the great victories of King Edward III, the Black Prince and King Henry V, not so many have heard of Sluys, and yet had the result there gone the other way, and it easily could have, England would have been invaded and conquered, the war would have ended and we would now be talking in French. It was a battle that the French could have, and should have, won, but due to a grave error of judgement on their commanders' parts they lost disastrously, the war continued and all its future battles would be fought in France, on enemy territory. The battle well illustrates the tactical competence of the young English king, Edward III, for it is a strange facct of medieval English kingship that occupants of the throne alternated between those that were utterly appalling, incompetent, capricious and downright unpleasant, and those who were just, militarily capable, strong and popular leaders. Edward III was unquestionably one of the latter, while his predecessor and successor both fell into the former category.

The result of the Battle of Sluys not only ensured that an invasion of England from the sea was out of the question, it also reinforced English ideas about land warfare, for it was a time when the old feudal system, that had endured more or less since the Norman conquest, was in steep decline and was being replaced in England by something that was truly revolutionary, and it was the victory at Sluys that convinced the doubters that the new ideas worked. Again, like the results of battles, there are few advances in warfare that are truly revolutionary — the chariot, gunpowder, barbed wire, battlefield aviation and atomic weapons are some, but there aren't many more. Sometimes it is a technological advance, sometimes a theory, sometimes — usually — a combination of both. Rarely is something that is truly revolutionary a 'light bulb' moment, nor even the product of one man or even one nation. More often it is a combination of ideas, experiments and experiences that may be spread over years and miles: the revolution occurs when all those ideas are brought together to produce something that almost at a stroke makes everything that went before obsolete. That was what was happening in England, reinforced by the result of the Battle of Sluys.

1 — Plantagenet England

The Plantagenets ruled England for 183 years. They were not a separate dynasty — the family had been the Angevins, but with the loss of Anjou by King John that soubriquet was no longer appropriate. When Henry III, the first Plantagenet, was crowned at the age of nine no one would have thought that his reign would last for fifty-six years. In 1216 the realm of England was riven by strife, with a significant number of the great men of the kingdom supporting a French pretender against King John, who although not as evil a king as history has made him out to be — monastic propaganda took its revenge for John's defying the pope — was pretty unpopular none the less. The death of John and the defeat of the pro French faction at Lincoln the following year took most of the steam out of the rebellion, and the magnates decided that an English king, however young, was better than a French one.

The French were bought off and most of the rebellious barons were pardoned. Henry survived his minority because he had good men about him who were genuinely concerned for the peace and stability of the kingdom and because most of the populace preferred legitimacy rather than civil war. Once he attained his majority and could rule in his own right a crucial factor was his agreeing to govern in accordance with the Great Charter, Magna Carta, which his father had signed but swiftly repudiated. His reign was not untroubled, but while there were frequent occasions when he attracted opposition by failing to consult the great men of the kingdom, he usually managed to compromise before opposition turned into rebellion. Such insurrection that did occur, particularly that of Simon de

Montfort in 1264, was put down, largely because it never attracted support from a majority of those that mattered.

Henry's survival depended not on popularity or even competence, for he had little of either, nor, in an age when kings were expected to lead their armies in the field, was he successful in battle, for his attempts to recover the French lands lost by his father were singularly unsuccessful. Eventually he had to accept the loss of Normandy and Maine, keeping only Aquitaine, but that as a vassal of the French king. Perhaps his main redeeming quality was that he was a patron of the arts and largely responsible for the promotion of what came to be known as the Gothic style of architecture. That he retained the throne until his death in 1272 was due partly to a reluctance in the country to revert to the constant endemic strife of the previous reign, partly because Henry accepted, reluctantly, that in England a king had to lead rather than drive, and partly because in the latter years of his reign the barons looked to his son, the future Edward I, whom they saw as a liberator and a reformer.

Edward I, thirty-three at the time of his father's death, was everything that his father was not. Tall, good looking, athletic, he heard of his accession on his way home from four years campaigning in the ninth crusade, where unusually he was an ally of King Louis IX of France. Having proved himself as a warrior, Edward's first task on reaching England was to order a root and branch inspection of the administration, resulting in fundamental reforms of what had become corrupt and weak governance. He removed dishonest judges, sacked avaricious sheriffs and ensured that the law was strengthened and enforced. While he was not averse to bending the rules to suit himself and his supporters, overall he provided the firm and generally just government that the nation needed. He pacified Wales, at least for a time, and began a process of Anglicisation that is still evident there today. In a series of campaigns in Scotland he removed the threat of border incursions and obtained recognition of the English king as overlord of Scotland, although the menace never really went away and would resurface after his death. He recognised that a king lacked the financial resources to rule alone and his reign saw increasing use of the assembly of lords and knights — now referred to as the parliament — who could agree taxation, something that inevitably increased to pay for Edwards' wars and his Welsh castle-building programme. A favourite ploy of medieval monarchs short of money was to levy a charge on the Jews, but by 1290 whatever riches the Jewish community may have had were gone, so Edward expelled them from England and turned to Italian moneylenders instead, running up massive debts by the time of his death. Despite this, all in all Edward, the 'Hammer of the Scots', was one of England's greatest kings — his eldest son and heir one of her worst.

Edward II was simply appalling. Capricious, dishonest, and uninterested in matters military, it was suggested by some that he might be a changeling, but in looks he was unquestionably a Plantagenet. Quite why great kings often produced incompetent and unpleasant heirs is a mystery. Perhaps the need to govern a kingdom detracted from the duties of fatherhood, and Edward I became increasingly autocratic as he got older, though it was the normal practice for a noble heir to be fostered with some great lord, so while parental contact might have been lessened, role models there were aplenty. Twenty-three when he came to the throne Edward II was uninterested in the business of kingship: he did not follow the expected pastimes of jousting and hunting, increasingly ignored the advice of his counsellors and seemed to be concerned only with his own pleasure and that of his companions. He had favourites, on whom he showered honours and riches that the increasingly unhappy nobility considered to be undeserved. He was homosexual, or perhaps bisexual, and his relationship with Piers Gaveston, a Gascon of undistinguished heritage, drew particular antagonism. Homosexuality at that time was not an offence under the civil penal code, but it was a heresy under canon law and generally disapproved of. Edward, and Gaveston, would probably have got away with it had they exercised a modicum of discretion but once Edward came to the throne he gave Gaveston titles that were normally reserved for members of the royal family. The marriage of kings was a dynastic matter, and whatever Edward's sexual proclivities it was essential that he married and produced an heir, so in 1308 he crossed to France to collect his bride Isabella, daughter of one French king and sister of three others. Edward further infuriated the magnates by appointing Gaveston as his regent during his absence. Gaveston himself might have lived to a ripe old age — he had no political ambitions — had he adopted a suitably subservient attitude to the great nobles, but when one is cleverer than ones elders and betters it is advisable not to make that obvious to them. Gaveston gave the various great men nicknames — often witty and appropriate, but also scurrilous — and made fun of them unmercifully. Not only that, but in the jousts and mock combats that were popular amongst the aristocracy, Gaveston usually beat his better-bred opponents. Inevitably there came a time when the lords had had quite enough of this Gascon counter jumper and he was kidnapped and murdered, an act which, to begin with at least, Edward was unable to avenge. Other favourites soon emerged, however, this time the father and son combination of the Despensers, both named Hugh. The Despensers were more dangerous than Gaveston, for they had political ambitions and the ability to pursue them. While the young Hugh was a more acceptable pet than

Gaveston, being at least of the nobility, the Despensers' amassing of riches and lands at the king's whim, and their arrogance, eventually provoked rebellion and the deposing of Edward, followed by his murder instigated, or at least condoned, by his wife and his son.

History has not been kind to Queen Isabella, only surviving daughter of King Phillip IV of France, and married to Edward II of England at the age of twelve or thirteen. Undoubtedly an adulteress, a rebel and complicit in the murder of her husband, she is stigmatised as the 'She Wolf of France'. In truth, however, she had much to put up with. She was past puberty on marriage and by all accounts was beautiful and intelligent, yet on the night of Edward's coronation he spent the night in Gaveston's bed rather than in that of his wife. Many of their wedding presents were given to Gaveston, and in what must have been a particularly humiliating bout of largesse, Edward gave the jewels brought over from France as Isabella's dowry to Gaveston as well. Despite all this, she was for many years a dutiful wife, producing the heir to the throne, the future Edward III, in 1312, the year of Gaveston's murder, followed by another son and two daughters.

Edward I on his death bed had commanded that his son continue the process of bringing the recalcitrant Scots to heel, an instruction that the second Edward largely ignored. By 1214, however, constant Scottish raids across the border, plundering of northern lands and levies laid on frontier villages had got to the stage where Edward II could ignore the situation no longer. Assembling an army by commission of array, where the magnates were required to fulfil their feudal duty by reporting with their followers ready for battle, Edward advanced into Scotland. Despite some of the barons failing to turn up on the grounds that the expedition had not been sanctioned by parliament, Edward's army was three times the size of that of his opponent's, Robert Bruce. Bruce was of Norman descent (the name had been de Brus) but the family had long been absorbed into the Gaelic nobility, and at the Battle of Bannockburn in June 1314 the English army was not only utterly defeated but routed, with Edward having to flee the field. The significance of Bannockburn is not only in the further damage it did to Edward's prestige, but as the catalyst for a revolution in the English way of waging war.

Scotland had been allied to France, England's traditional enemy, since Edward I's time, and any putative military action against France had to take into consideration the possibility of the Scots supporting the 'auld alliance' by attacking through England's back door — the Scottish border. In 1325, Edward decided to attempt to patch up Anglo-French relations by sending a diplomatic mission to Paris to negotiate terms that might lead to a lasting peace. The obvious person to head this mission was Queen Isabella, sister of the French King Charles IV. Previously a supportive wife to Edward, now the worm turned. Isabella crossed to France, taking her thirteen year old son, Edward Prince of Wales, with her and initially behaved perfectly properly, entering negotiations on behalf of the English king. Soon, however, it became evident that she had no intention of returning to England. She had tolerated Gaveston, who was careful not to offend her, but could not stomach Hugh Despenser and was genuinely in fear of him and his father. When Edward began to enquire when his queen might return she initially pleaded that negotiations were not yet done, or she was ill, or that she lacked funds for the passage, but eventually it became clear that she had no intention of returning as long as the Despensers were in power. Edward began to ask for, plead and then demand the return of Prince Edward, but as long as Isabella held the heir hers was the trump card. Her little court in Paris soon became the focus for discontented English exiles and she formed a relationship with Roger Mortimer, originally a friendship between two exiles in a foreign land but which quickly became sexual. Mortimer was everything that king Edward was not: strong, virile, a proven warrior — he had been a powerful lord of the Welsh Marches until taking part in an unsuccessful rebellion directed against the Despensers in 1321. A sentence of death was commuted to imprisonment in the Tower, but when it seemed that Edward might have him executed after all, he escaped and fled to France.

For a medieval married man to take a mistress was generally winked at, although the church officially disapproved, but for a woman to play the same game was a scandal, and if that woman was the queen it was not only a major scandal but treason too — two centuries later English queens would be put to death for far less. When the liaison of Isabella and Mortimer became public knowledge and attracted the condemnation of the pope, Isabella's brother, the king of France, could ignore it no longer and gave her and her lover their marching orders. While they were ordered to leave France the expulsion was unhurried, and their property, servants and ample funds provided by the king accompanied them as they moved to Hainault, in Flanders, where the count was sympathetic to their cause, such sympathy being reinforced by the betrothal of Prince Edward to the Count's daughter, Philippa. Now Isabella's court became not just a refuge for assorted exiles, but a centre for the plotting of revolt. Edward of England, having attempted to get Charles of France to cooperate in getting his son back (he had given up on regaining his wife) declared war on France in 1326, which only gave impetus to the plotters in Flanders, for now they could count on French assistance and funding, although Isabella and Mortimer drew the line at any suggestion of

French troops, as they well knew that this was the one thing that would unite England against them. Philippa's dowry was requested in advance, and used to hire 700 Flemish mercenary soldiers — said to be 'volunteers' — and sufficient ships to carry them, to be commanded by the Count's brother. Isabella's efforts to find, arm and equip troops could only have one purpose and could hardly be concealed from her husband's informers. King Edward sent urgent messages around the country: the navy was to be mobilised, coastal defences strengthened, magnates to summon their followers, soldiers to be arrayed. The response was hardly even half-hearted: in some areas it was ignored altogether, in others implemented only sufficiently to give the impression that the royal instructions were being obeyed. Edward was increasingly unpopular, unpredictable and ceding more and more power to the Despensers, while opinion amongst those that mattered was swinging towards Isabella.

A force of 700 hired swords, plus a few hundred English retainers of the exiles, albeit including a half-brother and a cousin of the king and two bishops, was a tiny force to invade a country of three million inhabitants, but it was all that Isabella could afford. There were insufficient funds to wait any longer, and in any case delay could allow Edward to root out her supporters in England. On 23 September 1326, in ten or a dozen ships — mainly wide-beamed cogs — the army set sail from Dordrecht, and a day later landed at the mouth of the River Orwell, near Harwich. Their crossing was smooth and not interfered with, as King Edward's fleet had mutinied and ships had dispersed to engage in the much more profitable pursuit of piracy along the French coast. The landing was in the territories of the Earl Marshal of England, Thomas Brotherton, first earl of Norfolk, son of Edward I out of his second wife, and half-brother of the king. Thomas had been badly used by the king, to the advantage of the Despensers, and while supposedly Edward's military commander for a wide swathe of counties, instead of opposing Isabella joined her. As the little army moved towards London more and more of the nobility joined them, particularly when Isabella ordered the plundering of manors belonging to the Despensers, but the respecting of property belonging to anyone else. Isabella, and her military commander Mortimer, had no wish to have to fight for the capital: to do would alienate the population whose houses would be destroyed or burned, and in any case fighting in built-up areas was something that all commanders attempted to avoid (as they still do), expensive on manpower and risking loss of control as it was and is. Isabella embarked on a sophisticated propaganda campaign: leaflets promising an end to tyranny and a restoration of justice, the removal of the Despensers and fairness for all. The replacement of Edward II by his untainted eldest son was never expressly stated — encouraging the removal of kings, even bad ones, by popular demand was not something to be encouraged. Initially Edward leaguered in the Tower of London, thinking that he could overawe the capital through his complacent lord mayor, but as more and more of his support melted away, either into the country until things died down, or to openly join Isabella, he realised that to stay where he was invited capture, and so he retreated westward, accompanied by the Despensers and a small retinue of those who remained loyal to him.

Now the London mob took matters into their own hands. Rioting broke out and those royal officials who had not fled were beaten up or killed, and if they had fled their property was ransacked. The mayor was forced to issue a statement in favour of Isabella and then deposed, the first task of his replacement being to release Isabella's other three children and Mortimer's many relations from the Tower. The archbishop of Canterbury, who had hitherto attempted to sit on the fence, issued a hurried proclamation in favour of Isabella and fled the city. Walter Stapleton, bishop of Exeter, was less fortunate. As the royal treasurer, responsible for tax collection, he was bound to be hated and when the Londoners caught him in the churchyard of St Paul's they wasted no time in hacking his head off, which they sent to Isabella as a token of their loyalty. Whether she personally opened this somewhat unusual gift parcel is not known, but in any event, having been assured that the city was hers she too moved westwards, pursuing the king. At Bristol fate caught up with the sixty-four year old elder Despenser, who was commanding a meagre rearguard to allow the king to escape into Wales where he was though to retain some support, and after a hurried trial where he was not permitted to state any defence, he was sentenced to be drawn, hung and quartered as a traitor and his head sent to be exhibited at Winchester. The rebels (although they insisted they were not rebels but simple 'contrarians') were anxious to act under the cloak of legality, and there was no precedent for the lawful deposing of a king. As it was rumoured that the king had fled by sea, and had therefore left the realm, allowing a regent to be appointed, on 26 October 1326, only a month after the landing, Prince Edward was proclaimed as Custodian of the Realm and writs issued for a summoning of parliament. Then it was discovered that King Edward had not left the realm after all — he had tried to but his ship was driven aground by contrary winds — so the Prince's writs were invalid, and it was the king who held the great seal of England, without the affixing of which no law could be valid.

Eventually the king and his entourage, now reduced to Hugh Despenser the younger, the Chancellor and a few retainers, were cornered in Neath abbey. The retainers were hanged out of hand, and after much haggling the great seal was handed over and the king, Despenser and the chancellor taken onto protective custody. The writs to summon parliament could now be sent out legally with provisions made for the king's inability or unwillingness to attend. Hugh Despenser was put on trial in Hereford on 26 November 1326. Condemned as a traitor, a heretic and a sodomite he was drawn to the gallows, hanged from a height of fifty feet, cut down and eviscerated while still alive, beheaded and his body quartered. His head was exhibited on a pike on London Bridge.

Now began a session of legal fudging over the person of the king. For the succession to be lawful the king had either to vacate the throne voluntarily in favour of his son, or he had to die, but that death had to be of natural causes. Mortimer tried to rely on popular acclamation and had the archbishop of Canterbury issue a proclamation stating that Edward II had abdicated in favour of his son, but this ploy failed when young Edward, rejecting the admonitions of Mortimer and his mother refused to meet the parliament until he could be assured that his father had willingly given up the throne and had done so in his eldest son's favour. After much toing and froing King Edward, faced with a choice of agreeing to surrender the crown or suffering he knew not what, gave in and Prince Edward was duly proclaimed as succeeding his father as Edward III, his reign beginning on 25 January 1327. As Edward, aged fifteen, was still in his minority, effective power would be in the hands of his mother, Isabella, as regent, who was increasingly under the influence of her lover, Mortimer. The problem now was what to do with the erstwhile king, for he still had supporters, and there were plots to rescue him and put him back on the throne. It was highly convenient, therefore, that the king, in custody in Berkeley Castle, died on the night of 21 September 1327, ostensibly of 'internal trouble during the night'. The body was exhibited, as it had to be to scotch any rumours that he was still alive and in hiding, and no marks of violence were seen. As Edward was only forty-three and had always been fit and in good health, a natural death is unlikely, and it is almost certain that he was murdered, probably on Mortimer's orders and with the connivance of Isabella. The tale that spread some time later that he was killed by having a red hot poker, or a tube of copper, shoved up his bottom is almost certainly false, and intended as an admonition against buggery, for burns to the buttocks would have been seen by those who had the task of embalming the body, and it is far more likely that he was smothered, which would leave no marks visible to the layman.

Then, in the following year, 1328, everything changed. Charles IV, king of France died, and with him the direct line of the Capets. France had seen five kings in fourteen years: Phillip IV died in 1314 and his three sons ruled after him. Louis IX died of pneumonia in 1316, his baby son, John I died aged five days, Phillip V, the second son of Phillip IV died of dysentery in 1322 and the third son, Charles IV died in 1328, probably also of dysentery. None of the three sons left any legitimate male heirs. But Phillip IV also had a daughter, Isabella, who had married Edward II of England and borne the man who was now Edward III. Edward III was Phillip IV's grandson and now his nearest surviving male relative. Isabella lost no time in lodging her son's claim to the French throne. While it was accepted that by French custom a woman could not accede to the throne, Isabella insisted that the claim could nevertheless pass through her to her son. The French nobility had already appointed a regent, Phillip of Valois, who was only a nephew of Phillip IV but of mature years and well-connected, and they were not prepared to accept the claim of an English king. It was this claim, which was only given up in

1802, that was to be the catalyst for the Hundred Years War and would lead directly to the Battle of Sluys.

2 — Preparations for War

Although Edward's claim to the French throne had been made, and rejected, there was little that could be done to enforce it for the time being. The removal of Edward II and his replacement by his son was generally welcomed, particularly when lands and titles expropriated by the Despensers were returned to their rightful owners and officials. Soon, however, all the promises made by Isabella and Mortimer began to sound very hollow indeed, as they began to implement the very abuses that they had promised to abolish. There were those who began to wonder whether the reign of Edward II was so bad after all. Matters were not helped by a resurgence of the Scottish problem, and an unsuccessful military expedition that resulted in the humiliating treaty of Northampton whereby Robert Bruce was recognised as king of Scotland. While Edward III had no part in the planning nor in the execution of the campaign, he was dismayed at its outcome, and it was at this point that he decided that he must escape from the control of his mother, and, by extension, of Mortimer. In 1330 Mortimer, acting in Isabella's name, summoned a parliament to meet in the castle of Nottingham in October. Isabella was now the Queen Mother, as Edward's wife Philippa had been crowned and had recently given birth to the man who would later be known as the Black Prince, but she was still the regent for the king. Security arrangements were tight: only the royal family and their immediate entourage would sleep in the castle, all others would, at the close of business on each day, repair to lodgings in the city and the castle would then be locked and guarded by men loyal to Mortimer.

On the night of 19 October a group of knights entered the castle by way of an unguarded (and presumably unknown to Mortimer's party) underground passage, met the king in the courtyard, killed the two knights on guard outside Isabella's apartment and burst in. The Queen Mother was in her bedroom while Mortimer and the treasurer, another bishop, were in the anteroom. Despite pleadings from Isabella to treat him gently, Mortimer and the treasurer were hauled off down the tunnel and into confinement in the town. Next morning, Mortimer's relatives and supporters were rounded up, and in November he and his two closest associates were sentenced unheard as traitors and hanged. Edward announced that henceforth he would rule with the advice of the great and learned men of the kingdom, and his mother was pensioned off into comfortable retirement. Edward's aim now was to reconcile the various factions and remedy the abuses that had caused strife and mayhem over the previous twenty years. There were no more executions; Mortimer's followers were treated lightly; a cursory investigation into the death of Edward II found no one culpable and the only person who might have indicated a trail leading to Isabella was murdered at sea. Edward did have to reward his adherents, but he was careful not to alienate others by doing so too generously.

Having appeased the nobility by a settlement that was as fair as it could be, given that lands and titles had been confiscated and reallocated by Edward II, then redistributed again by Mortimer, the eighteen year old king set out to re-establish law and order over the whole kingdom, where anarchy had ruled for years. Once again corrupt officials were weeded out and the king personally travelled around the country to hear the pleas of those who felt they had been wronged by the previous regime. During the rule of Edward II and later of, effectively, Mortimer, trust in the legal system had evaporated. Where a litigant thought that a decision of the courts might go against them kidnapping or even murder of judges was rife, and in many cases aggrieved knights and landowners would bypass the royal courts of justice altogether and seek a solution to a dispute themselves, usually by raiding their opponent's lands. Banditry was rife, with gangs living in the forests and preying on passing travellers, and although Robin Hood is a fictional character there were many like him, except that instead of robbing the rich to feed the poor they robbed everybody to enrich themselves. All this would take time to rectify, but slowly matters improved, with local magistrates made responsible for law and order in their areas, the appointment of judges unconnected with any particular faction and the passing of laws against hooliganism.

Meanwhile in France Phillip of Valois, now styled Phillip VI, was consolidating his position and the question of Aquitaine once more arose. The duchy of Aquitaine had been English since the future Henry II married Eleanor of Aquitaine in 1152, but its status was ill-defined: was it held by English kings in full sovereignty, as England claimed, or was it held as a fiefdom of the king of France, as the French averred? If the latter, then the king of England would be required to do homage – pledge loyalty – to the king of France, which English kings were reluctant to do, this reluctance leading to the confiscation of the Duchy on several occasions. Now Phillip was demanding that Edward of England cross to France to pay homage for the duchy. Edward was in no position to refuse: castles on the border of Aquitaine had been occupied by French troops; thanks to loans raised by Isabella the crown was heavily in debt to France, and the situation in England was still unsettled. In 1331 Edward crossed to France and went through the whole procedure of paying homage for Aquitaine, to the fury of his mother, now shorn of power, but objecting that Edward, the son of a king, should not pay homage to the son of a count. In French eyes Edward had sworn loyalty to Phillip, thus recognising that he held Aquitaine by Phillip's good grace. Edward's rationale was quite different: he had sworn loyalty not to Phillip personally, but to the king of France, and as he intended to claim the throne of France for himself in due time, restating the claim that his mother had made in 1328, there was no conflict in paying homage.

Edward III had every intention of enforcing his claim to the French throne but was as yet in no position to do so. Consolidation of his reign came first, and then there was the perennial problem of the Scots and their alliance with France. By a combination of luck and subterfuge the Scottish boil was burst, at least for the time being. A group of nobles who had backed the wrong horse in the struggle for the Scottish throne, won by Robert Bruce, and who had lost their lands in Scotland as a result, and who called themselves the Disinherited, cobbled together an army and invaded Scotland in order to place their candidate, John Baliol, on the Scottish throne. Edward made a great play of disapproval, forbidding the Disinherited to recruit in England or to cross English land, while at the same time providing them with clandestine support, for which Baliol had agreed to recognise Edward as overlord of Scotland. While all this was going on Phillip of France suggested that he and Edward should embark on a joint crusade. Edward professed that he would be delighted to participate but not just yet, as he was assembling an army for an expedition to Ireland. Edward was indeed assembling an army, but it was not for Ireland, and when Baliol and the Disinherited won their first tranche of battles he knew that he was no longer under threat from the back door. He took his troops not into Ireland but to Scotland and at the Battle of Halidon Hill on 13 July 1333 roundly defeated the main

Scottish army under Lord Archibald Douglas. Scotland secured, at least for the present, Edward returned to England.

In the 1330s England was in the middle of a revolution in her way of waging war. Previously the English military organisation, such as it was, was an amalgam of what the Normans did, imported after the conquest in 1066, and the Anglo Saxon system that had been there before it. Under this feudal system the king owned all the land, which he allocated to his great men, who in turn owed him military service when required. This service was generally for forty days, when the land holder was required to attend with a number of retainers depending upon how much land he held. These men, mostly knights or lords, or at least landholders, provided their own weapons and horses and had been brought up and trained to fight more as individuals rather than as part of a team. The quality and type of weapons varied widely, although lance and sword were the basics, the men could wear what they liked, and at the end of the forty days they could perfectly legally depart. These mounted warriors were backed up by the militia – the successor to the Anglo Saxon Fyrd – composed of the common folk who had little training and were not much more than an ill-armed rabble. They too could be embodied for only a fixed period – again usually for forty days. They could not be called out during the planting season and would have to be discharged before the harvest. This system was all very well for minor border disputes and dynastic squabbles, but was totally unsuited for anything that lasted longer than the forty days, such as a siege or a military expedition abroad, which increasingly English kings wished to embark upon.

The term revolution is over-used and frequently misused. It is very rarely the product of a lightbulb moment, nor of one individual, nor of one nation or even one continent. Sometimes the revolution is in ideas, sometimes in technology, sometimes in a combination of both. A true revolution is more often the product of ideas, experiments and inventions which may occur over a number of years in a number of areas. The revolution happens when all those ideas and devices are brought together to produce something that is so new that it makes everything that has gone before obsolete. In military affairs the chariot, gunpowder, barbed wire, submarines, military aviation and nuclear weapons were game changers, and while there may have been other developments that revolutionised the waging of war they have been a lot fewer than popular imagination might suppose. In England the revolution occurred over a period of about a hundred years, beginning with Edward I and reaching its apogee with the army of the Black Prince in the 1340s. The English revolution rested on three legs. The first leg was professionalism.

The feudal system was breaking down and no longer met what was required for English military campaigns. During Edward I's Welsh and Scottish wars both the king and some of his magnates began to recruit 'knights for pay' – that is men who contracted to serve for a laid down length of time for a specific rate of pay. This seems obvious today when the British army is made up entirely of men who voluntarily enlist for a specific period for a laid down salary, but it was not obvious in the thirteenth century. Since the collapse of the Western Roman Empire in the fifth century no one had professional armies: they may have had a handful of royal guards, like Harold of England's House Carls, but otherwise war was waged by feudal array or by men conscripted when needed – the peasant put down his hoe and picked up a spear when called out. Professional armies were – and are – expensive. If the pay is not attractive men will not join, and if conditions of service are not good they will not stay. The advantages of employing paid volunteers were of course enormous. Rather than turning up for forty days and going home again, professionals went where the king wanted them to go and could be trained to use standardised weapons and fight as a team. As the system of professionalism developed and more and more of England's soldiers became career warriors, a standard uniform appeared, so men knew exactly who was on their side and who was not. Initially this might simply be an arm band or a cockade worn in the helmet but as time went on it became a laid down pattern of armour or a jerkin of a specified cut and colour and a helmet issued to regulation design. A code of military law was devised, as it became obvious that the civil code was not designed to deal with military offences such as desertion or disobedience to orders.

The second leg of English professionalism stemmed directly from the first: professional armies are expensive, therefore they are small therefore technology is used as a force multiplier. Put simply if you are probably always going to be outnumbered on the battlefield you need to find some means of compensating for that, and in the case of the English it was the longbow. The longbow was England's weapon of mass destruction: consistently ignored by England's enemies, they were consistently massacred by it. Men had used bows and arrows for millennia and the Normans had archers at Hastings, but these men used short bows, a useful adjunct but not a battle winning weapon. The longbow was a very different proposition. As tall as the man who wielded it with a pull of anything up to 100 pounds and in some cases even more, it could propel a yard long arrow to a range of 300 yards, and go through an inch of oak at 100 yards. With a variety of arrowheads, some designed to go through flesh with barbs to prevent them being extracted, some with a needle-like point which would go through chain mail and even penetrate plate armour at short range, the longbow was a devastating weapon in skilled hands, and English archers were skilled, capable of shooting ten arrows a minute for minute after minute. There was a whole industry for making bows (made by the bowyers) and arrows (produced by the fletchers). Each arrow required three feathers which came from the pinion feathers of a goose. A goose has six pinion feathers, three on each wing, and if removed they grow again in the annual moult. Each goose therefore could provide for two arrows a year, and as various ordinances from the time of Henry III onwards made it compulsory for all males between the ages of fifteen and sixty to be in possession of a bow and a number of arrows, it is likely that the number of geese in the kingdom exceeded the number of men! It is probable that the longbow emerged as the result of experiment by hunters, rather than soldiers, and its range, accuracy and rate of fire would not be exceeded until the development of breech loading rifles in the 1880s, but whereas it took much practice over years to produce an archer, a man could be trained to use a musket in a matter of hours, which is why the bow and arrow ceases to be included in the equipment tables of English armies during the reign of Elizabeth I.

As time wore on the proportion of archers in English armies grew until by the time of Henry V they made up around two thirds of the army, although at the time of Sluys they were just over half the English strength. Although the Welsh made considerable use of archery in their guerrilla wars against the English, and Edward III had Welsh archers in his army at Sluys, archers were recruited from all over the kingdom, although it was said that the best came from Cheshire. While even before Sluys it was obvious to many French commanders just how dangerous English archers were, they could never persuade the French establishment as a whole to emulate them. French society was stratified to an extent that England's was not, and they retained a feudal system for campaigning, where the business of war was one for noblemen, with the lower orders there merely as an adjunct to the activities of their betters. Common men could not possibly influence the course of a battle, and that the English usually won the battles was attributed to their unsportsmanlike behaviour of employing ill-bred archers.

The third leg of the English military revolution was in the method of fighting. For centuries the mounted man had been king of the battlefield. Armoured cavalrymen had swept over Europe, not only the military superiors of the foot soldiers but their social superiors too – Equites, Chevalier, Caballero, Ritter, all titles that emphasised the position of the man on the horse. The infantry were mere humpers and dumpers, not much more than a moving fatigue party for the heavy cavalry of armoured knights, they could be scattered by a cavalry charge, hunted down and slaughtered. Then came Bannockburn, where Edward II's army of heavy cavalry had been roundly defeated by disciplined infantry who did not run, but stood their ground and presented a hedge of pikes, against which no horse would charge home. It was not only Bannockburn that changed English military opinion – there had been examples in Flanders of infantry defeating cavalry, but it was Bannockburn that acted as the spur for a change of tactics. Infantry, if it was properly disciplined, equipped and trained could see off any number of cavalrymen, however well-bred they might be. Put simply, no horse will gallop at something he cannot jump over or go through – go lickety-split at a hedge in the hunting field that your horse cannot jump and he will not go over it (although you might). From now on English armies would fight on foot, although they would move on horseback.

The English revolution in military affairs had arrived: a professional army that moved on horseback but dismounted to fight, which would form up in a battle line of infantrymen (men-at-arms), usually four deep, with the missile weapons, the longbows, on the flanks, and the horses tethered well behind. Ideally an English army would position itself on a ridge, where its flanks could be protected by a river or a wood or a steep escarpment, and allow the enemy to attack them, having to advance uphill to do so. From about 300 yards range the archers would start to deliver their arrow storm, shooting at a high angle so that the arrows came out of the sky with terrifying force. A thousand archers could deliver five thousand arrows in the first thirty seconds, and massed as the archers were, the cloud of arrows could hardly fail to hit something. While at extreme range the arrows would not pierce plate armour, they would deliver an almighty thump, would go through chain mail, strike the quarters and necks of the horses, and with a bit of luck some would go through helmet visors. As the charging cavalry got closer the archers would lower their aim and shoot horizontally, when if the strike did not go through the plate armour – and it often did – it would deliver enough punch to knock the man off his horse. Those attackers that survived the arrow storm and did manage to close with the infantry line met a solid wall of men-at-arms standing shoulder to shoulder and armed with a pole arm, a shortened pike around eight to ten feet long with a hook to sever reins and pull a man off his horse, a point to seek out weak spots in his armour, and a blade to hack. As the men-at-arms would now fight dismounted they had discarded the shield, and if they could not penetrate with the point they would try to knock the enemy soldier to the ground where he could either be despatched with a dagger thrust through the helmet visor, or given the change to yield – surrender – and ultimately be ransomed. This way of fighting was hugely successful throughout the Hundred Years War, although it did not happen all at once but over a period of time. Edward's army at Sluys was at a transitional stage, but the principle holds good.

The Scottish peace secured by the 1333 campaign was not to last for long. Opponents of Baliol appealed to Phillip of France for help to replace him with David Bruce, son of the ousted Robert. English spies reported that French ships were concentrating in the Channel Ports and that troops were being assembled in Flanders. French raids on English ports and coastal villages increased and state sponsored piracy operating from Calais increased. In 1336 another English expedition to Scotland was despatched, this time to render the likely French invasion ports unusable. Altogether three expeditions to Scotland were launched, and while the country was never brought fully to heel, it was at least rendered incapable of accepting a major French landing, although some single French ships with gold and weapons did get through. The French fleet that had been concentrated in the Channel ports to support a landing in Scotland was still in being, however, and it was clear that having been thwarted in Scotland, King Phillip was preparing an invasion of England. The winter of 1336 was full of omens: a comet blazed across the night skies – but what did it mean? A calf was born with two heads, flowers bloomed in January, there was panic along the south coast at the thought of a French landing and there was an orgy of beacon placement with churches ordered only to ring their bells in the event of invasion. In fact Phillip had missed his chance in the summer, and the onset of winter made the channel too unpredictable to risk his fleet, so the French held off and continued to build ships. On the premise that attack is the best form of defence, and with the threat from Scotland neutralised, Edward now began to prepare for war with France – but that required allies, and it required money. Flanders, now a republic having chased out their French count, was blackmailed into promising neutrality by the stoppage of English wool exports, and those duchies and principalities who were vassals of the Holy Roman Emperor, Ludwig of Bavaria, were brought on side by the promise of large grants of money. Hainault, whose earl was Edward's father-in-law succeeded by his son, Edward's brother-in-law, could be relied upon and the rulers of Brabant, Gueldres and Juliers were related to Edward or to his queen.

Money was another matter. Edward could raise a certain amount on his own behalf: customs duties had long been a royal prerogative, rents of royal demesnes were increased, loans from Italian bankers were negotiated, Cornish tin was appropriated, licences to mine for gold and silver were sold, speculation in the price of wool was engaged in and even Edward's own crown was pawned, but this was never going to be enough, so unless parliament was to be summoned and asked for yet another grant on top of the ones granted for the Scottish campaigns, a quick victory was needed. In 1337 Edward once more declared himself to be the rightful king of France and on 16 July 1338 with his fleet and his army Edward sailed from Walton on the Naze and landed in Antwerp. The start to the campaign was inauspicious, the promised allied contingents were not ready, and although Edward and his entourage did meet the Holy Roman Emperor in Cologne and was promised his full support, the nearest the English came to a decisive battle was on 23 October 1339 at Buironose, when having agreed to do battle the French king thought better of it and withdrew. On 23 January 1340 in the main square of Ghent, Edward announced his claim to the French throne. It was an empty gesture. His expedition had so far achieved nothing, he was rapidly running out of money and his creditors were closing in. Only by the leaving of the Queen and her children in Antwerp and the pawning of her crown could Edward secure the agreement of his creditors and as yet unfunded allies to his returning to England to obtain more funding. It was not a good start to what became the Hundred Years War.

3 — To War

Medieval English kings were not all-powerful. Most of what they did required money, and once a king had exhausted his own resources (rents of royal lands, customs dues, sale of monopolies, loans from bankers and the like) he had to raise funds from taxation of the populace, and this could only be granted by parliament. Parliament was not, of course, a body elected by universal suffrage as it is today, rather it was a gathering of those who mattered: the nobility in the House of Lords and increasingly the 'knights of the shires' in the House of Commons – men drawn from the English counties and who could speak for that county. When parliaments acceded to kings' requests for money they normally exacted a quid pro quo, which might be the abandonment of some royal perquisite or means of raising funds that parliament did not approve of.

Even before Edward's return to England Parliament had been considering his requests for more money. Their meeting in February was acrimonious, and although the Lords granted a tax of one tenth on themselves, that is a tenth of the value of all funds and moveable property, the Commons demanded concessions in kind. They wanted a committee set up to oversee the spending of taxes granted, and an investigation into past diversions of taxes into purposes other than those for which the money had been voted. If these requirements were not met then a tax would not be approved. These demands were unheard of, and when conveyed to Edward, who was still in Flanders, his representatives replied that if the tax were not provided than the defence of the coastal areas against French raids could not be guaranteed. Reluctantly the Commons agreed a contribution of 2,500 sacks of wool. It was not going to be nearly enough. It was not only the financial problems that upset Parliament. In his absence in Europe Edward had rather lost touch with popular opinion at home, and his proclamation that he was the rightful king of France was not received with the joyful acclamation in England that he had hoped for and expected. France was England's traditional enemy, the Lords resented the sequestration of English lands in France and the common folk living near the coast were the subject of French depredations, raids and burnings. The English saw themselves as free men and looked upon the French as oppressed subjects of uncaring autocrats. Parliament insisted on an act that said that at no time and under no circumstances could any Englishman be subject to the laws of France.

Edward landed back in England on 21 February 1340 and Parliament assembled on 29 March. The king took his place on the throne in the House of Lords, the Commons were summoned to attend and the Chancellor, the Archbishop of Canterbury, made a plea for funds. Should the money not be forthcoming then the kingdom and the country would be lost, the king would have to return to Brussels to be imprisoned until his debts were paid, his honour would be forfeit and the nation left defenceless. On the other hand, if the monies were forthcoming, the king had a strategy that would put his enemies to flight and restore the prosperity of the kingdom. Faced with this Parliament could do little else but agree, and they granted a generous one ninth on the country and one tenth on the clergy for two years, but not without conditions, which were very similar to those the Commons had demanded in February. Additionally they repeated that at no time should they be required to obey Edward or his successors in their capacity as kings of France. Given the situation that he was in,

Edward had no option but to agree – he needed the money and he would accept whatever conditions came with it, however irksome they might be.

If Edward was to take not only funding to repay loans but a sizeable army back to France, he would need ships to do it, but England was not a naval power and it would be several centuries before Britannia would rule the waves. Although English kings had long proudly proclaimed themselves to be 'Lords of the English Seas', with Admirals of the North and the South reporting to them, by Edward III's time this was empty bombast. The admirals were either soldiers, who might know quite a lot about fighting on land but little or nothing about naval warfare, or great lords who knew little or nothing about any kind of fighting, while the Royal Navy was a handful of cogs in harbour with masters but no crews. English naval policy was concentrated on protecting wine convoys from Bordeaux and even these were subject to piracy from Calais or raids by French ships. For anything more ambitious ever since Edward the Confessor (1003 – 1066) the Royal Navy was supposed to be augmented from the Cinque Ports (Sandwich, Dover, Romney, Hythe and Hastings with Rye and Winchelsea) in exchange for various customs and taxation exemptions. The trouble was that since the Confessor's time some of these ports had silted up and with the exception of Dover were no longer of much importance as centres of maritime trade, Yarmouth and Southampton having long eclipsed them. Apart from that, many of the ships which were supposed to be earmarked for the Royal Navy were in fact fishing boats or cargo vessels, unsuited for battles at sea. Edward now sent his commissioners around the country requisitioning ships and ordering them to south coast harbours to be fitted out for war. Most of these were cogs, with a wide beam and a shallow draught, built of oak and of anything from ten to 200 tons displacement with a single mast and a square sail. They were not particularly manoeuvrable in a contrary wind, but they could stand rough seas, albeit producing very uncomfortable conditions for the occupants, and could get up rivers and into small harbours that ships of deeper draught could not. In the River Thames were the nine ships of the so called Royal Navy, while the Cinque Ports reluctantly mustered twenty one ships at Winchelsea and Edward's commissioners collected more to be concentrated at Portsmouth. Most were merchant ships about sixty feet long and twenty wide.

Turning English ships originally designed to carry freight into warships entailed erecting 'castles' front and rear, that is wooden towers from which archers would shoot at enemy crews, and crows nests, platforms near the top of the mast which would hold two or three archers and a lookout. Additionally various pieces of artillery were placed on board the larger ships: mangonels (a type of catapult), and trebuchets (a form of sling using a counterweight) both of which shot a round stone projectile and springalds (a crossbow type device which shot a large iron bolt to a range of about seventy-five yards). While these instruments could theoretically be operated from on board ship, the chances of hitting anything were low and their prime purpose was to augment sieges on land. One ship was ordered to carry the enormous quantity of thirty-two tons of gunpowder, which would indicate that at least one of the ships was to carry some form of primitive cannon. Stalls for horses had to be made and accommodation for the crew (usually around twenty sailors) and the soldiers provided. All over England forests were being cut down to modify the existing sequestered ships and to build more, while at the same time crews were being impressed and soldiers assembled.

By now everyone in an English army was paid, from the earls downwards. Archers were either contracted to the king directly or under a commander who contracted either to the king or to one of the nobility. A vintenar commanded twenty archers, the equivalent of a modern platoon commander, and a centenar, today's company commander, had five vintenars and their men under his command. Men-at-arms, the infantry, were members of a retinue, that is employed directly by the king or more usually by a lord or a knight, and the size of retinues varied from a dozen to several hundred. Eventually Edward was able to assemble an army of around 5000 men, in the proportion of three archers to two men-at-arms, accompanied by the usual administrative officials, clerks, farriers, grooms and surgeons. Later in the war all archers would be mounted, but at this stage not all were, and those without horses attracted a lower rate of pay than those with. Archers were not only cheaper than men-at-arms but cost less to equip, needing only a helmet and a leather jerkin, rather than expensive armour. Once they had expended their arrows they could be used as light infantry and mounted archers could be used in a scouting and reconnaissance role. A hurried visit to Yarmouth managed to procure some more ships, making a grand total of around 160 ships to carry the army and its horses and stores.

If England was not a maritime power, France most definitely was, with her major shipyards at Rouen on the River Seine and ships designed for fighting and others designed to carry troops. French warships were mainly galleys, little changed from classical times and powered by oars with a lateen sail which would be used when cruising. A lateen sail was triangular and allowed a ship to sail into the wind. A typical gallcy was long and narrow, propelled by thirty oars on each side, each oar manned by three marines. The ship had a ram at the front and the tactic was to ram an enemy ship and then board, the boarding party being two men from each oar, leaving one man per oar to provide some steerage. These galleys were highly manoeuvrable, regardless of the wind direction, and could turn in their own length. It has been calculated that they could maintain a steady speed of around seven knots, with ramming speed, which could only be kept up for a short time, of ten knots. Not all galleys were French, for a number were contracted from the Republic of Genoa and had been moved up from the Mediterranean. The number of galleys the French could muster was slightly reduced when a spy reported that eighteen were beached at Boulogne, preparatory to being moved up to Flanders, and an English raiding party landed and burned them. Nevertheless, what they did have were far more manoeuvrable and suitable for fighting at sea than the clumsy English cogs.

French troopships, for transporting the army, were either modified merchant ships reliant on sail alone, or clinker-built Norman barges with oars and a square sail, this latter only allowing sailing with the wind behind them but still more easily manoeuvred than anything in the English fleet. The converted merchant ships had castles fore and aft from which crossbowmen could shoot at the crews of enemy ships. The French had never taken to archery – the idea of armed and disciplined bodies of Frenchmen from the lower classes of society would be seen as a threat to the established order – so they employed large numbers of Italian mercenaries armed with crossbows. This weapon loosed a metal or wooden bolt, known as a quarrel, to about the same range as the longbow when shot in a flat trajectory but unlike the longbow it was ineffective in the indirect role when shot at high angle. Unlike the longbow it could be used by almost anybody, and at short range its penetrative power against plate armour was probably better than the longbow's arrow. It was, however, more expensive to produce than the bow and due to the time needed to reload had a much reduced shooting rate – perhaps two quarrels a minute compared the ten arrows a minute that the longbowman could loose.

Phillip of France had originally assembled a fleet to take an army to Scotland, but that had been scuppered by Edwards forays against the likely landing areas. Now that fleet would be augmented to invade England directly and the expedition would be launched from Sluys, a port that is now silted up but was then at the mouth of the Rivers Zwin and Honde and was the main port for Bruges, at the mouth of the River Scheldt downriver from Antwerp. Ships were moved from Boulogne and other French ports to create what Phillip called The Great Army of the Sea and consisted of six galleys, 22 oared barges, seven sailing ships specifically built as warships, 167 merchantmen modified as troopships and a number of other vessels from the Mediterranean, augmented by a number of Castilian battleships, great towering three-masted monsters with castles that overlooked any English ship. Manning the fleet were around 20,000 men, soldiers and sailors, but this is less imposing than might appear, for of the army only 150 men-at-arms were experienced soldiers, who acted as the officers, and there were but 500 hired crossbowmen. The remainder of the army was made up of militia, partly-trained and ill-equipped, and recently impressed recruits, hardly trained at all. The nobility, regarding sea battles as beneath them, were conspicuously absent. Once the invasion force had landed in England the feudal array would follow and take the glory.

Activities on both sides of the channel could not be concealed. Phillip knew very well that an English army was being assembled, and equally Edward was aware that the French were planning an invasion. The answer, in Edward's eyes, was to forestall Phillip by striking first, and the army was ordered to assemble and embark with the ships then rendezvousing off the mouth of the River Orwell. Inevitably, given the slowness of communication over bad roads and none, there were delays. The king wanted to sail at Whitsun, the first week of May in 1340, but it was not until well into June that the ships were ready and the men embarked. During this time French raids continued, the Channel Islands, Winchelsea, Folkestone and Southampton all had visitations by French raiding parties who landed, looted, burned and sailed away. Many of the members of Edward's council, including the chancellor, were against the expedition: there was an enormous French armada waiting for him; the Scots might yet launch an attack across the border; the coastal towns would be left defenceless, but Edward was adamant. He really had no choice: parliament had voted the money to equip the fleet and pay the soldiers and sailors, and keep the debtors at bay. Not to go would not only leave his reputation at home in tatters and render him completely unable to raise loans ever again, but to fail to turn up would mean the imprisonment of the queen and the internment of his soldiers left behind in Flanders. His advice rejected, the chancellor resigned, but as he was replaced by his brother the protest can only have been nominal.

In France too funds were needed, but whereas England had been a united country with a central government since the reign of Alfred the Great's grandson, Athelstan, in the mid tenth century, the king of France ruled directly only what is now called the Isle de France, or the area around Paris. The rest of the country consisted of a number of Duchies — Normandy, Brittany, Burgundy, Artois, Aquitaine, Anjou, Touraine, Blois and Toulouse — each with their own duke, who nominally owed fealty to the king. How strong this fealty was and how much it was paid depended upon the power of the king: a strong king with a sound treasury could usually depend upon the obedience of the dukedoms, where the king was weak or impoverished, the dukes went their own way. Aquitaine was of course claimed by the English in full sovereignty, whatever the young Edward may have said, no doubt with fingers firmly crossed behind his back; Brittany was often in open revolt, and later on for much of the war Burgundy would side with the English. Unlike in England, where taxation was resented but accepted, albeit grumblingly, the French were not accustomed to heavy taxation, and Phillip's commissioners had to plead and negotiate to raise the money needed to fund the coming war. Only the inhabitants of northern France took the threat of an English invasion seriously, and the towns and cities did agree to provide cash. Paris made a large grant and the church also contributed, encouraged by the pope who had declared himself for the French on the grounds that Edward's coalition included the Holy Roman Emperor, Ludwig of Bavaria, who had been excommunicated as a result of territorial squabbles in Italy and Ludwig's attempts to depose one of the pope's predecessors. The pope's support for France only reinforced English suspicions of the papacy, which they considered to be under French control, as indeed many popes were.

Having raised the funds and assembled the fleet and the army, Phillip was faced with a number of options. He knew very well that an English army was embarking for the continent, and he could either blockade the embarkation ports and prevent Edward from ever putting to sea, or he could intercept the English fleet at sea and destroy it, or he could allow it to begin to land and then attack it when it was most vulnerable. One of the problems that the French faced throughout the war was one of divided command. Wars and battles cannot be run by committee: a commander must be appointed, told what the king or government wants him to achieve and then allowed to get on with it. A good lesson, rarely learned by kings and politicians from the earliest times to the present day, is that they should tell a commander what to do but not tell him how to do it. In this case the French Great Army of the Sea had no fewer than three commanders, two French admirals and a Genoese mercenary. Huges Quiéret, fifty years old in 1340 and a nobleman who had served as grand chamberlain and grand master at the French court was created Admiral of France in 1335, the first Frenchman to hold a post previously held by contracted foreigners, usually Italians. He quickly showed himself to be a good organiser, improving the running of the dockyards and reforming the system of obtaining naval stores. That he had some seagoing experience was evidenced by his command of a raid on Southampton, when his men landed, looted, pillaged, raped and sailed away again unmolested. His fellow Admiral of France, Nicolas Béhuchet, appointed in 1337, was described as a 'short fat Norman of low birth' and owed his appointment more to his talents as a financier, able to negotiate large loans for Phillip, than to any military ability. He too, however, did have some experience having commanded a French squadron that captured an English convoy taking wool to Flanders in 1338, although his massacring of the prisoners was regarded as straying well outside the conventions of war. In the French military hierarchy both the admirals ranked below the Constable of France, who in 1340 was Raoul of Valois, Count of Eu and a military nonentity who acted purely as a mouthpiece for his relative, Phillip, who himself had little strategic understanding. The third co-commander was a highly experienced Genoese mercenary, whose name is given variously as Pietro Barbanero, Barbenoire, Barbevaire or

Barbavera and who was a veteran of naval battles in the Mediterranean and of raids on English ports. He had brought with him a number of Genoese galleys and was a far more experienced seaman than either of the two French admirals. Having put Quiéret, Béhuchet and Barbavera in command of the fleet and its embarked army, Phillips instructions to them were stark: they were to hold the borders of Flanders, prevent the English from landing and prevent them from taking any port in Flanders. If they failed in this, went on Phillip's letter, they would be executed!

On the evening of 21 June 1340 King Edward III boarded the cog *Thomas*, now his most powerful ship since the previous flagship the *Christopher* had been captured in a French raid. Prior to going on board he had made arrangements for the governing of the country in his absence. The regent, in theory at least, would be the ten year old Prince Edward of Woodstock (later the Black Prince) advised by a picked council of experienced royal servants. Some ships would be left behind to defend the south coast and there were instructions to guard against any interference from Scotland. At first light the next morning, 22 June, the fleet sailed, and while the earl of Warwick was the admiral in charge, Edward stated that when the fleet came into action he would take command, so important was the occasion. As Edward was a bad sailor and was frequently seasick, this was a risky decision to take. Also risky was Edward's decision where to head for. He knew that the great French armada was at Sluys and that he was outnumbered, both in ships and in men. Assuming the French fleet stayed where it was and did not put to sea he could have headed for Ostend or Dunkirk, where he could have hoped to land unopposed and then attacked the fleet from the land side. An attack on land would mean he would face a disembarked French force of perhaps 15 or 16 thousand with his own 5,000, but Edwards men were professionals and would be fighting amateurs, so the odds were perhaps not as bad as they might have seemed. If, on the other hand, the French fleet put to sea, Edward's best plan might have been to avoid it and land either at Sluys or any other port on the Flanders coast. In the event he decided to head straight for Sluys, and while in hindsight we know he was right, it was a brave, and perhaps foolhardy, decision at the time, made against the advice of his experienced officers, but showing great confidence in the abilities of his sailors and soldiers.

Unbeknownst to Edward, the French commanders had made their decision. Quiéret and Béhuchet did not get on personally. Quiéret thought his fellow admiral an ill-bred opportunist, while Béhuchet thought Quiéret an arrogant dilettante. Neither had much regard for the abilities of the other. On one thing they were, however, united – they would not risk the fleet and hence their own necks. The safest thing to do was to stay put and blockade the harbour, thus preventing the English, when they came, from landing. That Edward might alter course and head for a different port does not appear to have occurred to them. Barbavera, the only real warrior of the three, was appalled. He urged the two admirals to put to sea and intercept the English fleet. He pointed out that not only had they considerably more ships and men than did their enemy, but they had galleys and oared barges that were far more manoeuvrable than anything Edward had. The French ships could split up the English squadrons, attack them under oar power from any direction and defeat them in detail. Those ships not sunk would be taken as prizes and the English king, if not killed in the battle, taken as a prisoner to Paris. The French were far better sailors than the English, and more capable in fighting on the sea, it would be madness not to capitalise on that. His pleas fell on deaf ears. He was little more than an unwashed pirate – what could he possibly know?

The English fleet approached the Flemish coast in the late morning of 23 June. They could see the French fleet and it looked formidable. Edward ordered his ships to heave to and sent a small party of knights including John Chandos and Reynold Cobham ashore. They were landed at Blankenberg, twenty miles west of Sluys, by long boat with their horses swimming behind them. Their instructions were to scout out the French dispositions, count the number of ships, estimate the number of men and see in what formation they were arrayed. At the same time the bishop of Lincoln and his horse were put ashore with instructions to ride to Bruges, about ten miles away, and encourage the inhabitants and the garrison to attack the French from the land, to coincide with Edward's attack from the sea.

By early next morning, 24 June, King Edward knew what he faced. All was ready for the battle that would change history.

4 — Into Battle

Having decided, against the advice of the only real expert in naval warfare, to block the mouth of the river leading to Sluys and let the English enemy attack them, the two French admirals had arranged their fleet in three lines, from the little island of Cadzand to the mouth of the harbour. In the first line were their largest ships, including huge Castilian vessels, some from Flemish loyalists and, with a deliberate snook to the English, the captured cog *Christopher*, originally the flagship of the Royal Navy. The sides of the ships had been boarded up with planks of wood, to present a great wall against boarders, and in each line the ships were chained together, to create, as the admirals hoped, an impenetrable obstacle. On the fore and stern castles were massed the crossbowmen, nearly all in the first line, while the soldiers and marines stood ready to repel any attempt to board. The English would find themselves opposed by a mighty wall of ships, would be subject to a hail of crossbow bolts as they approached and if they got anywhere near the French first line would dash themselves to destruction against it. So was the thinking of Quiéret and Béhuchet, who were increasingly irritated by the insistence of the hired Genoese, Barbavera, that it would not work. He reiterated that the French should make use of their ships' ability to manoeuvre, put out to sea and attack and destroy the English fleet as they tried to make a landing. As before, he was ignored. The French ships had been put in position the previous day, 23 June, and since then the tide had changed several times, with the result that the ships had drifted eastwards and were fouling each other and pressing up against the island of Cadzand. Quiéret ordered the chains to be removed, but there was still very little room to manoeuvre and there was much shouting and cursing as ships impeded each other as they tried to return to their assigned places.

Meanwhile Edward knew very well what was going on within the French fleet. Chandos and Cobham had returned from their reconnaissance on land, and Sir Robert Ufford, who had preceded the fleet with a few ships, had carried out a thorough examination of the coastline north and south of Sluys. These men were typical of those who would make their names and fortunes in the war, for unlike in France, where position was largely decided by birth, English society was mobile, with men advancing, or declining, on the basis of their ability. Reynold (or Reginald) Cobham had served at sea (he would later become Admiral of the West), and in the army and he had been employed on several diplomatic missions when Edward was negotiating, or pretending to negotiate, with Phillip. John Chandos had come to the king's attention at Cambrai in 1339, when he defeated a French knight in single combat, a foolhardy but effective way of gaining attention, which in this case worked as Chandos was knighted shortly afterwards. Robert Ufford was a younger son with little prospects when he became a soldier in 1324 at the age of twenty-six. He supported the opposition to Edward II and then sided with Edward III against the Mortimer faction. He served in Gascony against the French and in the Scottish wars led a retinue of forty-three men at arms.

Aboard the *Thomas* King Edward gave out his final orders to the ships masters and officers of the army who were rowed across in ships' boats. The English fleet was anchored about three quarters of a mile off Blankenberg, and there were two important criteria for a seaborne attack on Sluys. Firstly, as the English ships relied on square sails they needed the wind behind them, and secondly it would be an advantage to have the sun behind them to blind the French crossbowmen. The wind was blowing from the north-west, and in a few hours the sun would be in its midday position, exactly what Edward needed. He ordered that the fleet would move up and then turn towards the French, with the ships in three lines abreast. The first line would have one ship of men-at-arms flanked by two containing archers, a total of twenty ships of infantry and forty of archers. The second line would have around forty ships, mainly of men-at-arms, while the third line, the reserve, would have thirty or so fighting ships and also, closely protected and held in rear, the transport ships with the horses and the military stores, the treasure and, crucially, the wives of officers and ladies-in-waiting going to join Queen Philippa.

Edward himself would command the first line in the *Thomas*, whose master was the redoubtable John Crab or Crabbe. Sixty years of age in 1340 Crab was probably born in Flanders and after learning his trade as a seaman became a highly successful pirate, being particularly adept at attacking and capturing English ships. During the Scottish wars he effectively commanded the Scottish navy, running the English blockade, and on the English withdrawal become Constable of Berwick. When Berwick was recaptured by the Disinherited and Baliol he was forced to flee and was eventually captured in battle by the English. Parliament wanted him put to death for numerous acts of piracy but King Edward could see the man's ability and paid his ransom. The fact that the Scots would not (or could not) pay his ransom, coupled with a generous offer from Edward persuaded Crab to turn his coat and henceforth he became a loyal servant of the English king. When Berwick had yet again to be retaken from the Scots his intimate knowledge of the town's defences was particularly useful and soon he became Edward's trusted flag captain. Admiral Thomas Beauchamp, eleventh earl of Warwick, who would command the second line, although only twenty-six at Sluys was already an experienced soldier and sailor, while the reserve would be under the leadership of Robert Morley. Aged forty-five at Sluys Morley was another experienced soldier and sailor who had served in Scotland as a man-at-arms in the retinue of his uncle in 1314 and was present at the disaster of Bannockburn. He campaigned actively against Edward II and supported Edward III's taking power from Mortimer. Employed to command English naval sorties against the French coast he was now Admiral of the North, and although he had advised Edward against the venture he served loyally and competently in it.

Just after midday the English fleet was in position, about a mile off Sluys and the signal to advance was given. With a gentle wind behind them the three lines of cogs moved at a stately walking pace towards the French. With only square sails to rely on, keeping in line was not easy and much shortening and then increasing of sail, and in some cases the deployment of sea anchors was needed to maintain formation. From Edward's flagship, the *Thomas*, flew the Royal Arms of England, which now included the French fleur de lys, quartered with the lions of England, to display Edward's claim to the French throne. What particularly annoyed the French was not Edward's use of the fleur de lys – as the grandson of one French king and the nephew of three others he was entitled to have it on his escutcheon – but that it was quartered subservient to the English lions. How, they asked, could a mere offshore island consider itself superior to the great empire of France? Soon both sides could clearly see each other: the great French vessels of the first line still struggling to return to their assigned positions, with much trumpet blowing and shouting, to which the English replied by blowing hunting calls.

As the distance between the two lines narrowed, the archers on the forecastles and crows nests of the English ships strung their bows and placed their quivers of arrows where they could conveniently be reached. Then, when the French line was around 400 yards away the centenars and the vintenars gave the order: 'nock' – each man selected an arrow and notched it to his bowstring. 'Draw' – and each man's bowstring was pulled back level with his right ear with his left arm fully extended. 'Loose' – and the first volley of arrows shot into the sky, and the orders came again, rapidly this time – 'Nock, 'Draw', 'Loose' as the arrow storm was launched on the helpless French, still too far away for their crossbows to have any effect. On the French decks the effect was devastating. Coming out of the sun like an iron hail storm, something like fifteen thousand arrows came hurtling down in the first thirty seconds, and against the packed French ships could hardly fail to hit something. At this stage the archers had no specific target, they merely aimed to hit the French ship in front of them and as their decks were packed with men, many without plate armour, casualties began to mount. Another fifty yards and the English ships came within crossbow range, but with the sun in their eyes aiming the crossbows could only be approximate, and as the crossbowman had to put his foot in the stirrup at the end of the stock and lever the bowstring back into the shooting position after each discharge, the rate of around two quarrels a minute was no match for the longbow, even if there had been more crossbowmen.

As the range shortened even more the archers began to target the crossbowmen directly. Many of them, hired Italians looked down upon by their French employers, quickly realising that they were on the losing side of the missile battle, abandoned the unequal struggle and hunkered down behind the boarding on the sides of the ship and stayed there, oblivious to the kicks and shouts of the French men-at-arms. By now the range was down to a hundred yards or so and the archers switched to aiming at the sailors and soldiers on deck. Using bodkin arrows – needle pointed to go through chain mail and, at this range, plate armour too – and broad heads with barbs designed to pierce flesh and be difficult to extract, the numbers of the dead and wounded on the decks of the French first line began to mount. A small mercy was that on this occasion the archers did not poison their arrows by dipping the head in human faeces, but even so the wounds were shocking enough. The French attempted to use their stone throwers against the English ships, but these weapons were highly inaccurate at sea and most stones simply fell into the water. Another reported French tactic was to hurl dried peas at enemy decks, supposedly making it difficult for the crew to run (which sounds unlikely), and to shoot bolts from springalds, again with little success.

And now, at around 1500 hours, the English ships crashed into their French opponents. This was where the English were most vulnerable, for their tactic was to use grapples to bind the ships together and then to board, using grappling irons with ladders attached. The French ships in this first line were all much higher than those of the English – the massive *Saint Denis* carried 200 men – and although the French soldiers had suffered greatly from the arrow storm, if they could prevent the English from boarding and board their ships in turn, then the day would be theirs. It was not to be. While the castles on the English ships were lower than those on the French ships opposing them, their crows nests were high enough for the archers there to hit any man who tried to get to the side and cut the grappling irons. Under the cover of the archers enough English soldiers got up onto the decks of the French ships of the first line, and once there they could hold the defenders off until more men got on board. From now on the battle became a hand to hand fight between the English men-at-arms and the French militia and pressed men, with a scattering of armoured knights in command. The English were hard-bitten professionals, they had fought the Welsh, the Scots and the French before, and they had one commander – the king – who boarded and fought with them. The French on the other hand had forfeited their numerical advantage by splitting their fleet and those manning it into three, and by blockading the bay as they had, were unable to use their ability to manoeuvre. Their soldiers and marines were largely inexperienced and for many of the pressed men their hearts were just not in it. French command was divided and the three leaders were in dispute amongst themselves, while the one real naval warrior – Barbavera the Genoese – had no faith in the plan from the outset.

In war on land soldiers who were losing could always run away, but on a ship there was nowhere to run to. On land a man-at-arms, who was often a knight or someone who wanted to be a knight, had a fair chance of surviving a battle provided he was not mortally wounded or killed in the fighting, for if he yielded – and surrender was perfectly honourable if there was no way to fight on – he would be taken prisoner and then ransomed. The ransom would be a sum of money depending on the prisoner's rank, or if the prisoner had no money it might be land, or horses, or armour, or, if all else failed, working for the captor for an agreed period. It was in the interests, therefore, of a fighting man to take prisoners and to treat them reasonably, for income from ransom was the captor's pension. The so-called code of chivalry laid down all sorts of provisions intended to regulate warfare and dealt with the treatment of civilians, women and prisoners. If the prisoners were not worth ransoming, however, all bets were off, and in this battle most of the French were impoverished commoners, who could not possibly have raised a ransom. No quarter was given therefore, and the battle became a slaughter, with the defenders being killed outright, their only escape being to jump into the sea. Most of those who jumped and wore armour sank to the bottom and drowned, those who were not armoured and who could swim – and this was not an age when everybody could swim – and who got to the shore were then murdered by Flemish civilians just waiting for the opportunity to revenge themselves on the French interlopers.

By about 1800 hours, after three hours of savage fighting, the French ships in the first line began to strike their colours and the English were through. Of particular joy was the recapture of the *Christopher* and three other English ships that had been lost to French raids, the *Edward*, the *Saint George* and the *Black Cock*. Edward had been wounded with cuts to the thigh and hand, but not seriously, and he now ordered the second English line to take possession of the defeated French ships and put crews upon them, while he would take the first line on to deal with the French second line. As these instructions were too complex to be transmitted by trumpet calls or flags, a knight was sent off in a longboat to convey them to Beauchamp, commanding the second line.

In the French second line, composed of the smaller vessels, panic was setting in. They could see the colours of Phillip of Valois hauled down from the mainmast of the *Christopher* and replaced by the lions of England, and the realisation that the Great Army of the Sea was not, after all, invincible, began to hit home. This time, as the two lines closed, the advantage was with the English, for now their ships were higher than those of the French, and the arrow storm and boarding were faster and even more disastrous than in the first phase of the battle. A few brave Frenchmen who survived the archers resisted and fought bravely, only to be slaughtered by the English men-at-arms whose blood was up and who threw those they wounded overboard. At this stage it was clear to the watching Flemings that the French were beaten and they now sallied forth in their own small ships and attacked the French ships from behind as the English closed from the front. The bishop of Lincoln's harangue to the men of Bruges bore fruit as they arrived and began to kill any Frenchman who managed to swim to shore.

The ships in the third French line, composed of the oared Norman barges and a contingent from Dieppe, did not stay to fight but tried to escape round the east side of the island of Cadzand and out into the north sea. Now the battle developed into individual skirmishes, ship against ship, as the English tried to prevent the remnants of the French fleet from getting away. Some of the Norman barges made it, but many of the Dieppe contingent, reliant only on sail, were overhauled by English ships and grappled. As night fell the fighting died down, but some individual contests went on all night. One relatively tiny English ship, funded by the priory of Christchurch in Canterbury, had taken on the Dieppe flagship, the mammoth *Saint Jacques* and had become inextricably entangled with it. As the two ships drifted round Cadzand the English boarded, slashed their way across the deck and then returned to cut their own ship free to avoid running aground. When the English boarded the wallowing *St Jacques* again next morning they counted 400 dead Frenchmen.

For many medieval battles the actual details of the fighting are obscure, but Edward III was an inveterate report and letter writer, many of which survive. Although he could speak, read and write English he normally wrote and spoke to his lords and knights in Norman French, the language of the nobility and the educated, while the language of the common folk was what we now term Middle English, known to us from the writings of the contemporary Geoffrey Chaucer. That within sixty years English kings and nobles spoke English in preference to French was all part of the sense of English separatism encouraged by the war. In addition to Edward's reports there are numerous accounts of the battle both by English and by French chroniclers, and although medieval numbers of participants and deaths tend to be exaggerated (overstating the strength of the enemy and understating one's own made victory seem even greater) we can form a reasonable estimate of the results of Sluys. For the French it was a total and unmitigated disaster. Of over 200 French ships involved the English captured 190 of them. Edward sent John Crabbe and a detachment of ships after the Norman oared barges that had fled, but able to move against the wind they got away. Barbavera took his galleys and escaped, no doubt mouthing 'I told you so' to any Frenchman who might have been inclined to listen. For days dead bodies came floating ashore and as the English massacred all on a ship once boarded, the French death toll may have been as much as sixteen or seventeen thousand. Neither admiral survived. Quiéret was either killed in the battle or executed afterwards (by beheading as befitted his rank) while Béhuchet was recognised and taken prisoner, his captor hoping for a fat ransom from this financier-turned-sailor. No ransom was collected however, for King Edward was not prepared to allow the man who had been the scourge of the English seashore to live, and he was hanged from the yardarm of his own ship.

For the English the butcher's bill was 500 or so killed, mostly during the boarding of the first French line, and perhaps 1500 wounded. While at this stage of the war most English men-at-arms wore chain mail, with only a few in the more expensive plate, they were still reasonably well protected and most of the wounds would have been cuts and bruises which, as long as they did not become infected in the unhygienic living conditions of the time, would result in a speedy recovery. Nevertheless, the dead amounted to ten percent of the army so was not negligible. Only four officers were among the dead, Thomas de Mouhermere, Thomas de Latimer, John Butler and Thomas de Poynings, the descendants of the last three making frequent subsequent appearances in English military and political history. That night there was great celebration aboard the English flagship, and elsewhere in the fleet. Those who had done well in the fighting and whose actions had been noted by the king or senior commanders were knighted, others were made monetary grants and a mass of thanksgiving was said. Next morning Edward received the mayor and aldermen of Bruges, and two days later made a pilgrimage on foot to an ancient church nearby. Next day the army was on the move again, on land this time, to Ghent, where the king was reunited with Queen Philippa, no longer in peril of imprisonment for debt.

The news did not take long to reach Paris, but to begin with nobody was prepared to tell the king. Eventually the court jester, who could get away with much that others could not, turned the result of a battle into a joke: why, he asked the king, were French knights braver than English knights? The answer, he said, was that English knights did not jump into water in full armour. Soon the search for the guilty and the apportionment of blame began. The dead Béhuchet was castigated for his low origins and accused of trying to save money by not employing enough men-at-arms; the Normans, whose boats had got away crewed by men of little account, were base cowards, while Barbavera must be arrested for treason. It was a year before Phillip reluctantly agreed that perhaps Barbavera was not entirely to blame, and the appearance of Norman survivors some horribly mutilated did convince the king, although not his court, that the loss of so many Norman ships and many of her menfolk should attract pity rather than blame. As would be emphasised more and more in the years that followed, defeats, claimed the French nobility, were solely due to the treachery and or incompetence of the lower orders of society, and not the fault of the French military system. The English victory at Sluys seemed to presage further disaster, and the coastal provinces were demanding protection, with reinforcements being rushed to ports where the local authorities thought the English might land next. That there was only one English army and that was with Edward had escaped the notice of the French.

Edward's despatches reached London on 28 June, but even before that rumours had spread of a great English victory. When the news was confirmed national joy was unconfined. Services of thanksgiving were held in all parish churches, the victory despatch was read in all town squares, the taxation and hard times of the past were all worth it. Some years later, when the national coffers were full again, a special gold florin was minted in honour of the victory. Englishmen had always been distrustful of foreigners and now nationalism and a sense of superiority, already nurtured by the Scottish wars, began to grow. The doubts about Edward's kingship and his qualities as a war leader evaporated overnight; for the moment at least he would find it easier to persuade Parliament to authorise taxation to fund him, and in the meantime the sale of the captured ships and the ransom of the few (very few) French officers that had been captured rather than killed and kicked overboard, would go some way towards replenishing the English governmental coffers.

5 — The Battle That Changed History

With uncharacteristic modesty, King Edward attributed the English victory to God's favour. Whether he really believed that or not, in a god-fearing age when the church held considerable influence it was probably a wise enough statement. The truth, of course, was somewhat different. The French had failed to capitalise upon their own strengths: they were a naval power with more, bigger and better ships than the English. They should have, and could have, put to sea and fought a sea battle, which they would have won. Instead they allowed the English to fight a land battle on the decks of ships, and the English were very much better at land warfare than the French were. The French command was divided. The two admirals disliked each other and neither was prepared to serve under the other. The result was a compromise, what they thought was a safe option, and their decision making was not helped by the king's assurances that if the English were allowed to land or to capture a port, both admirals would answer for it with their heads. The only sensible voice was that of Pietro Barbavera, commander of the Italian galleys, who rightly saw that the French had ships that could manoeuvre regardless of wind direction, and that they had far more vessels of every description than the English. That his advice, based on wide experience of sea battles, was ignored was partly due to his being a commoner (although so was Béhuchet), and partly because as a mercenary who fought for hire rather than for a cause, he was not entirely trusted – he was being paid to fight for France, but what if he had secretly accepted a better offer from Edward of England?

By taking up a static position blockading the bay of Sluys, the French forfeited the ability of their oared galleys and barges to move in any direction, and by dividing the fleet into three lines they threw away their numerical superiority – although of course there was not room to put all the ships in the front line – and handed the initiative to the English. In the battle of missile weapons 500 crossbowmen were simply not enough to take on 3000 archers. 1000 quarrels per minute against 30,000 arrows could not possibly neutralise the archers, even if the sun in their eyes had not made aiming difficult for the crossbowmen. To produce anything like an equivalent barrage would have needed 15,000 crossbowmen, and even if that number could have been found it is unlikely that there would have been enough deck space to accommodate them. The 500 that the French did muster were mainly Italian mercenaries with a few Frenchmen and were regarded as being near the bottom of the social pecking order. They were unlikely to risk their own lives to an extent over and above the strict limits of their contracts.

There were not enough experienced men-at-arms to command and control the French soldiers and marines aboard their ships, and while the sailors were highly competent at sailing their ships, the soldiers were largely ill-trained and many were only recently impressed. Infantry was in any case not highly regarded by the French, who believed that battles were decided by mounted and armoured knights, and while the few men-at-arms were not mounted they might have put up a better defence had they fought as a team rather than as individuals. The English on the other hand were professionals who fought as teams under recognised sergeants and officers, and they had plenty of practice. Both English infantry and archers, although also paid to fight, had a cause that was worth risking their lives for, and they had one commander – the king

– whom they admired and respected and who shared their dangers. It was certainly a huge risk to attack the French fleet head on, but Edward had weighed the odds and he was proved right.

Had the French done what they could and should have done history would have been changed irrevocably. If the French fleet had put to sea and intercepted the English expeditionary force there can be little doubt that the English ships would have been scattered and the fleet defeated in detail. King Edward, had he not been killed, might have been captured and hauled off to Paris in chains. The French fleet could then have gone on to effect a landing in England where there was very little to oppose them. In conjunction with their reinvigorated and encouraged Scots allies they could well have taken London and declared Edward III deposed, and replaced him with one of the many claimants, or even by Isabella, ensuring a French client upon the English throne – they might even have given the English throne to David of Scotland, son of Robert the Bruce, who was married to Edward's sister Joan. Exiled from Scotland as children, David and Joan had been brought up in France, under the influence of Phillip VI, until the Francophile David was reinstated as David II in 1336. Even if Edward was not declared deposed, the ransom demanded would have been enormous, and the English magnates might or might not have agreed to pay it – and even if they did agree the time taken to raise it and the suffering it would cause to the populace might well have ignited revolution. Whatever the decision as to the English throne, there can be little doubt that the Hundred Years War would never have happened and France would have dominated England for the foreseeable future. Even if King Edward had managed to get away from his defeated navy and get back to England, his reputation would have been in tatters, his credit non-existent and his wife imprisoned for non-payment of his loans. As it was, the English victory at Sluys meant that the coming battles of the war would all be fought on French soil, with French towns and villages, and French peasants suffering the destruction, the burning, the pillage and the massacres, and not English ones. French lands would be laid waste, and not English ones. The threat of a French invasion of England was now no more, and would not re-emerge for another four hundred years.

In the immediate aftermath of the battle it seemed that it would be but the start of a glorious and successful summer campaign. Hainault, only a lukewarm ally since the death of the old duke, Edward's father-in-law, found its enthusiasm for the cause rekindled, the pope was persuaded to lift the interdict on Flanders and withdraw the excommunication of the Holy Roman Emperor, Ludwig of Bavaria. Edward set off to besiege Tournai in the hope of drawing Phillip of France into a major battle, and Robert of Artois, allied to Edward because of French support for a rival claimant to the dukedom of Artois, was sent off to take St Omer. In an age before effective artillery, which could blow holes in high walls, a medieval fortified town or castle hardly ever fell to assault. There were only three ways in: over by ladders, or siege tower; through by battering ram and under by tunnelling. All of these took a great deal of time and were risky options. Sieges were won by starvation when the besieged garrison ran out of food or water; disease whether naturally occurring or induced, or treachery where an occupant was bribed to open the gates.

Things now started to go wrong. Tournai was strongly fortified, well stocked with food and Edward had only the few siege weapons that he had brought with him, not nearly enough to pose a threat to a city like Tournai. Phillip with a French army advanced as far as Bouvines, about ten miles away, but thought better of it and withdrew; at St Omer Robert of Artois was making no progress and his Flemish soldiers deserted him; the funds that Edward had brought with him had all been expended in paying his allies and the interest on loans and he was now in urgent need of more, and once more the Scots were resurgent. If things were not going as well for the English as might have been hoped, they were equally unfortunate for Phillip, whose army was camped around Lille where its soldiers were dying in their hundreds from 'fever'. As Lille then was surrounded by marsh this was probably malaria. When emissaries from the pope arrived to suggest a truce, both leaders accepted with relief. In September it was agreed to suspend hostilities until midsummer's day 1341, to apply also to Scotland. Later this was extended to June 1343 with all prisoners being released subject to their ransoms being paid and the county of Ponthieu, subject to the duchy of Aquitaine, being returned to Edward. In November Edward, his queen and two youngest children returned to England, which took him three days in the teeth of a gale. While he found public opinion strongly behind him as a result of the victory at Sluys, that did not extend to willingness to provide more money and Edward's savagely quick temper was expended on the government, whom he blamed for not providing sufficient finance. Not only, in the king's opinion, had the administration failed to raise the taxes to which he was entitled, but on investigation it was clear that some of the monies that had been raised were creamed off by corrupt officials along the way. He now began a root and branch clear out of the administration. The Chancellor, the Archbishop of Canterbury, the equivalent of the modern prime minister, was summarily dismissed and lucky not to be executed, and replaced by the first secular holder of that office. When civil service priests pleaded clerical immunity he sacked them, and as the king's committees of enquiry roamed the country looking at accounts, peculators in public office and extravagant administrators were replaced. It is surprising, with such a wide ranging upheaval, that the administration continued to function at all, but it did, largely because the common people and the less influential knights and merchants were not displeased to see proud officials humbled.

Edward Plantagenet is today regarded as one of our greatest kings, and he is a fascinating character. Fair, just, incorrupt and a sound administrator he had a notoriously quick temper, although it disappeared almost as quickly as it arose. Although he had Mortimer and his two closest adherents executed, Mortimer's other supporters were in most cases forgiven, and even Mortimer's grandson was, eventually, restored to the king's favour. He was politically astute and the problems of 1340 on his return from Europe after Sluys reminded him that the power of an English king was not absolute. He made a point of calling parliament regularly and keeping that body informed of his thoughts and intentions, and not just when he needed money, as for the next few years of his reign he assuredly did. On the darker side, while he may not have been personally complicit in his father's murder, he made little effort to find out what actually happened, although in fairness he had been under his mother's sole influence from the age of twelve, and Isabella had been treated so appallingly by her husband and his favourites that Edward can have had little love for his father. Although he eventually turned against his mother, so completely under influence of Mortimer as she was, her banishment was one of considerable comfort and in due course she did occasionally appear at court, although no longer wielding the levers of power.

As arguments about funding went on, and as people at home seemed to derive no practical benefit from the victory, the importance of Sluys began to fade. The rest of the campaign achieved little and the French king resisted all temptation to face the English in open battle, including turning down an invitation from Edward to face him in single combat. Only three years after Sluys the general view was that the campaign had been an expensive failure. And then in 1345 things changed for the better: in a lightning campaign an English army under the Earl of Derby recaptured most of Aquitaine from the French. Edward now felt able to ask parliament for the money to take an army to France and continue the war.

The army that Edward took to France in July 1346 was entirely professional, and almost entirely mounted – they would move on horseback but fight on foot. Landing near Cherbourg on the Cotentin peninsula in Normandy Edward led his army east, burning and plundering on the way. The aim was partly economic – destroy the enemy's ability to raise taxes by destroying anything of value – and partly to terrorize, thus making the point that Phillip of Valois was unable to protect those who he claimed to rule. If the main French army and the French king could be tempted into battle on ground that suited the English, to settle the war and Edward's claim to the throne once and for all, so much the better. In late July the army captured Caen by assault, unusual at the time but made easier by the city walls having been allowed to fall into disrepair. They moved along the Seine, almost to Paris, and then headed north, crossing the Somme on 25 August at Blanchetaque near Abbeville. Then, followed by a French army getting bigger and bigger each day, Edward and his army reached Crécy en Ponthieu, and on 24 August took up a position along a ridge, with two divisions of men-at-arms forward and one, commanded by Edward in person, in reserve at the rear. The archers were positioned on the flanks.

Edward's army at Crécy probably totalled 4,500 armoured infantry and 3000 archers, with several thousand Welsh spearmen – light infantry who acted as scouts and looked after the baggage and the horses.

During the late afternoon of 26 August the French army with its various contingents began to close up on Crécy, where they could see the English army drawn up in a defensive posture. By a conservative estimate the French, with Phillip himself present, mustered around 30,000 armoured cavalry and up to 2000 crossbowmen. Again, there was no clear chain of command, as although Phillip was the nominal leader each of the many nobles and royal relatives present wanted a say. Phillip's preferred option was to wait until the following day when yet more French allied troops would arrive, but with the crowded ranks in the valley and more and more pressing forward to look at the enemy, and where instant obedience to orders was an unknown concept, Phillip had to accept that he could not hold his men back any longer and so the battle might as well begin. At around 1700 hours the crossbowmen were sent forward but had little effect, not helped by a sudden rainstorm that soaked the bowstrings and loosened them, and they were further written off when the front rank of mounted nobility rode over this band of low-born mercenaries and galloped up the hill, anxious to get at the English. The result was disaster for the French. Those that survived the arrow storm and the ditches dug as traps for the horses were no match for the English men-at-arms in their disciplined formations armed with vicious pole arms. Time after time the French charged and time after time they were beaten back, until as darkness fell they had had enough and the French king and his entourage fled the field.

The well-known and often-told tale of the sixteen year old Prince of Wales, in nominal command of the right-hand division of infantry being hard-pressed with his father, the king, declining to send support and commenting 'let the boy win his spurs' is almost certainly nonsense, albeit a good story all the same, as is the death of the 'blind king of Bohemia' who had only one functioning eye but was certainly not blind. The French losses were enormous – at least 2000 of the nobility and an unknown number of crossbowman killed – while English losses were less than 200. Edward marched on and then laid siege to Calais, with the intention of starving the garrison out. Meanwhile the French had implored their ally, the Scots, to do something to distract the English and in October 1346 the Francophile King David II led a Scottish army into England. The Scots had miscalculated badly and at the Battle of Neville's Cross, north of Durham, on 17 October 1346 they were roundly defeated by the garrison of York commanded by the Warden of the North, the church militant in the person of the Archbishop of York, and King David carted off to the Tower of London.

The siege of Calais was a long and tedious business, not concluded until August the following year. This, however, was a real bonus for England. Calais had long been a centre of piracy preying on English convoys to Bordeaux, but also further afield, and the city was stuffed with years of plunder. With the huge sums of money realised by the ransoming of French nobles and knights taken in the approach to Crécy and the battle itself, and now the capture of riches rarely seen before, it was Crécy and Calais that occupied the minds of those at home, and not Sluys. With the return of the army it was said that there was not a woman in England who did not wear something – a jewel, a brooch, a rich robe – that had come out of Calais. Edward was greeted with acclamation and parliament agreed that the money for the campaign was well spent. The king founded the Order of the Garter, of twenty-six members headed by himself, who had distinguished themselves in battle. Today it is the oldest order of chivalry still in existence, although its members no longer have to prove themselves in battle.

Joy and avarice was short lived, however, for in the following year, 1348, the Black Death, the plague, reached England having raged through Europe from Sicily via Marseilles. The Black Death killed at least forty percent of the population, perhaps fifty percent in some places, and there was little time for campaigning by English or French. The effects of the plague were much worse in France than in England, for in England, a unitary state, the administration did not break down, and government, albeit with great difficulty, still worked. That was not the case in France where all social order broke down, not helped by the number of government officials killed or taken prisoner at Crécy.

It was not for another seven years that a major expedition could be sent to France, this time under the command of the twenty-five years old Prince of Wales, Edward the Black Prince, who achieved another great victory at Poitiers on 13 September 1356, which resulted in more slaughter of the French nobility and the capture of the king, now Jean, son of Phillip of Valois. Once again there was celebration in England but still no sign of the end of the war, which dragged on punctuated by truces of various lengths, in which the English won all the battles but could not bring the French government, even with their king a prisoner in the Tower, to the table. The Black Prince aged only forty-six died in 1376, probably of amoebic dysentery (although malaria is a possibility) and his father Edward III followed him the following year, aged sixty-five and senile, but still revered for what he had been.

Once again a strong and capable king was followed by a weak and incompetent one in the shape of Richard II, son of the Black Prince, and once again English attention looked inwards and not to France. Richard was deposed in 1399 by his cousin, Henry Bolingbroke, son of Edward III's third son, John of Gaunt. Richard was subsequently murdered and Bolingbroke ruled as Henry IV. His reign was punctuated by rebellion and risings in Wales, and there was little time for adventures in France. It was not until his son, Henry of Monmouth, came to the throne in 1413 as Henry V that the claim to the French throne was restated, with Henry taking an army to Harfleur in 1415. That campaign led to another stunning victory, that of Agincourt on 25 October 1415 when a half-starved, sick and exhausted English army defeated a far larger French feudal host, at minimal cost. Once again the combination of disciplined infantry supported by archers won the day and now the French at last recognised that they could not win this war and given that their present king, Charles VI, was mad they would have to come to terms with the English. Henry was recognised as the regent of France and as heir to the throne on the death of Charles. To seal the treaty Henry married Katherine of Valois, daughter of Charles.

With the great victories of Crécy, Poitiers and Agincourt, and the capture of Calais, which remained in English hands for over 200 years, and now with the settlement of the inheritance question, Sluys receded even further in public consciousness. Everything changed on the untimely death of Henry a mere seven years later, leaving the child Henry VI as his successor, followed by political wrangling at home and a resurgence of French resistance south of the River Loire. Only forty years later England had lost all that had been gained in the war with the exception of Calais, as dynastic squabbles, later termed the Wars of the Roses, once again turned English military efforts inwards.

The Hundred Years War turned Anglo Normans into Englishmen, speaking and writing English rather than French, and men of Anjou, Burgundy, Artois and the rest into Frenchmen. A country of three million was never going to be able to hold a country of sixteen million by force of arms alone. The English won all the battles but they simply had not enough men to hold the territories they conquered. Sluys became a forgotten battle and in most accounts, including modern accounts, it has only a passing mention, if mentioned at all, and yet it was the critical battle of the war. Had England lost Crécy, or Poitiers, or Agincourt, they would simply have gone home. Had they lost Sluys, which could so easily have happened, then English, and European, history would have been changed for ever. It really was a battle that changed history.

ENGLAND EXPECTS: THE BATTLE OF SLUYS

If you enjoyed *England Expects* check out Endeavour Press's other books here:
Endeavour Press - the UK's leading independent publisher of digital books.

For weekly updates on our free and discounted eBooks sign up to our newsletter.

Follow us on Twitter and Goodreads.

Printed in Great Britain
by Amazon